The book of poems *Girl in Tuli[* ... ...* healer. The chronicle of a mother who has lost her daughter to illness, the poems bring her daughter to a beautiful presence in the space of memory that is marked in equal measure by loss and by the need to hold on to every living moment. Both daughter and mother become mythical in their suffering and their battle with the process of dying: they gather the characteristics of creatures from the natural world that will serve to put life and death in perspective.

Every poem is a gift, but "The weight of not knowing," where the daughter runs from one bookstore to another and brings to her mother a heavy atlas, asking her to "hold this," because it contains "all the places you want to go," represents one of deepest expressions of bewilderment and longing I have ever read. The final poem in this book, "Portable family," brings the expression of loss to its most palpable and yet most spiritual:

> [...] the agonizing absence presses
> On the brick that was your heart

"Talitha Cumi," inspired by Christ's words to Jared's daughter, ends with the prayer that animates this extremely powerful collection:

> "Oh, let her rise golden from this drying earth
> And leave us not as rust, not ember, nor dearth."

CARMEN BUGAN
George Orwell Prize Fellow
and author of *Poetry and the Lanugage of Oppression*

DiNenna's volume takes on the imperatives of motherhood through the immediacy of individual moments. Her clear and cogent lines achingly detail the pain, perils, and helplessness of standing witness to a child's cancer. The poems heartbreakingly hold on for dear life but, even more heartbreakingly, demonstrate the need to let go into living.

DR. JEANA DELROSSO
Sister Maura Eichner Endowed Chair of English,
Professor of English and Women's Studies,
Notre Dame of Maryland University

*Girl in Tulips* is a guide for the gut disguised as a poetry collection, written from the heart of a mother who's explored myriad paths through the loss of a daughter—including horoscopes, a priestess, Greek mythology, the Bible, wildlife, and time—to the heartfelt realization that "when children leave, they take you with them."

ELIZABETH BOQUET
author of *Galoshes*

Charged, stark and elegiac, DiNenna's debut collection is an unflinching exploration of the relationship between mother and teenage daughter, a dynamic that is both constrained and strengthened by the daughter's cancer diagnosis. With great clarity, these poems provide a lens on how a mother's love negotiates the quotidian of their child's journey. A sharp eye for image, a honed ear to the sound of loss and grief, these deeply felt poems are full of fierce hope, faith, healing, and acceptance.

MARY-JANE HOLMES
author of *Set a Crow to Catch a Crow* and *Don't Tell the Bees*

Julianne DiNenna is a storyteller first and foremost, her stunning narrative poetry imploring us to listen, to pay attention. And we can't help but do so. Her use of language is both beautiful and surprising, every word carefully chosen, every shared moment something sacred. Her grief is ours, her memories our own. DiNenna's *Girl in Tulips* is a moving collection that holds us close and breaks our hearts.

HANNAH GREICO
editor of *Already Gone: 40 Stories of Running Away*

Julianne DiNenna's poignant collection *Girl in Tulips* interweaves the fecund mythical realm with that of the sterile medical theater, arriving at a hybrid world populated by supernatural beings in white coats who hold in their hands the complicated threads of human lives. These poems echo Demeter's lament for her lost daughter, tracing the footsteps of a grief-stricken mother through a cancer ward in which "emptiness is its own universe." We witness her bargaining with an array of implacable divinities, her rare moments of joy in the midst of despair, and the aftermath of her unimaginable loss in which she turns to words to make sense of the chasm cleaving her life in two. In times like these, language becomes essential to our survival, and memories achieve the status of constellations because "we must choose the flickerings we hold onto." *Girl in Tulips* gazes unflinchingly upon illness and caregiving, anguish and tenderness, grief and loss, and the countless myth-imbued mysteries of our aching, extraordinary lives.

ROMANA IORGA
author of *Temporary Skin*

Oh God, how this collection aches with loss, love, the unimaginable re-imagined into these poems for a baby girl, a wish for her to come home for a spell, the spell being each line, each lyric, an incantation that does indeed bring her home.

RANDALL BROWN
founder and managing editor of Matter Press

# Girl in Tulips

and Other Non-Communicable
Family Diseases

Julianne DiNenna

**Fernwood**
PRESS

# Girl in Tulips
## and Other Non-Communicable Family Diseases

©2023 Julianne DiNenna

Fernwood Press
Newberg, Oregon
www.fernwoodpress.com

Printed in the United States of America

Cover and page design: Mareesa Fawver Moss
Cover photo: Lisa Verena Pape

ISBN 978-1-59498-114-2

To my three daughters, it is an honor to be your mother

# Table of Contents

# Acknowledgments

"Lemons" and "Olive Oil" first appeared in *Gyroscope Review* in January 2016.

"Gifts to Myself" was published in *Adanna Literary Journal* in 2018.

"Send Out the Clowns," "Searching for Next Dave Brubeck," and "Demi Sings Us Taps" appeared in *Jerry Jazz Musician* 2019 and 2020.

"I Want Cake" appeared in *Poetry Shed* 2019 and in *Poetry X Hunger* 2020.

"Ward Moms" was published in the *Journal of Compressed Creative Arts* in September 2020.

"Effervescence" was published in *And If That Mockingbird Don't Sing* in 2022.

"Mother's Day" was published in *Literary Mama* in 2022.

"Portable Family" appeared in "A Portable Paradise Prom(pt)," ebook inspired by Roger Robinson.

If I can stop one Heart from breaking
I shall not live in vain
If I can ease one Life the Aching
Or cool one Pain
Or help one fainting Robin
Unto his Nest again
I shall not live in Vain.

Emily Dickinson 1830–1886

# Spring

# Mother's Day

Here at the sidelines a very different game:
    the court stretches the range of the neighboring forest,

past the creek, back along the street. In the pizzeria, mothers
    raise glasses of red wine, toast sport kids and fertility,

imbibe themselves silly, their spouses drink beer. Winter retracts
    its tentacles to the mountain edge. In the waning frost,

the cold ground folds into white starched walls. I follow
    swirling blue lights honing on an H lighthouse

landing pad, some teenage girl tottering on a crutch
    knocks me into the revolving door.

In the waiting room, soccer splays on big screens,
    a whistle blows like a train alert at a trail pass.

A baby asleep on the faux-leather couch, her mother
    re-packs her overnight bag. I wade down the corridor

find you in a barren room. Alone. A doctor parachutes in,
    her theater scrubs filled with air, a phone clipped to her ear.

Snowy strobes on a gray screen, some strange birthing,
    a double, doctor's pen circles a cloudy,

spiked-ball flail marble. These walls separate night air,
    distant pines, the oak lit up in the playground.

Then the touch of a nurse's hand, a voice asking what faith
    I profess. I stare at your orchid face, this bud

of fifteen years I once soothed to sleep, I once walked to school,
    I once warned of boys. Where is that ball

to hit my head, to wake this lioness to a nighttime game of life
    vs death, to breathe fire, to keep the night from chasing the day.

Sekhmet's priestess drags a chair close, takes my daughter's hand,
    flips through her prayer book, a whistle in her mouth.

# Things that Flash

Your gold earrings
Glittery pink polka-dot pencil case
Sparkly hair clips
Fluorescent pink backpack

Glints of light rebound
I remove your earrings from your earlobes
Barrettes from your hair
Stuff them into your pencil-case
Drop them into your backpack

The red light on the heart rate monitor
The blue light of the drip
Shine from the drip pouch

Kisses on your pink cheeks
Flickers from the surgeon's blue surgical scrubs
*One last kiss*, she tells me

*Do a good job*, I tell the surgeon
Her blush under the surgical mask
Silvery wheels of the gurney thrust into motion

All the yellow messages flaring across the phone screen
I have no strength to answer

# Waiting

comes down a dispenser
a coin away
coffee as fresh as plastic can hold.
The pretend plant will not get
the air cleaner, yearning
for your first post-op cry
when your eyes pry open, tear
your lips part.

The street beyond the window
where fields once bloomed
trams pass, mothers push strollers,
metal fuses with plexiglass, asphalt rips in heat,
horns honk, rubber tires skid at the cross-walk,
some God-believing man hollers at the lady behind the pram.
She cannot be remote-controlled, she lashes back.

The coffee spills around the rim of the cup.
Waiting for you to re-emerge
you will be filled with plastic tubing
the splinters of your head plastered
under bandages and gauze,
I plead the posters of past pastures on the wall
tell me the password to your portable
the location of your id card, your bus-pass
and all other non-essential miscellanea one doesn't need to know
while leaning my head in the crook of my arm
against the glass of the beverage dispenser
planted next to the emergency room door.

# Pass Over

Nightmares or
upset tummies or bike-splats that brought
broken saucer sores or
brush burns that illuminated shins the way
lightning woke you in hours unknown to young age,
tiny fingers laced my neck,
ankles hooked around my hips,
your chin zipped to my shoulder,
a nose locked into my hair,
those sacred seconds you wore me
in your arms of God's promise,
like lamb's wool
till I was not your draped altar but more so a relic
that had to be minded
suddenly all that
passed over, passed over.

When a buckle busted in your head,
they pried, they jabbed out fragments,
needled and sewed, riveted your skull.
Blue surgical suits wrapped and re-wrapped your head,
a tightly knitted bow the color of wash water
and delivered you in stitched cloth.
Through swollen eyes
I plead Heaven to lock you in yourself,
pull you toward the womb that once housed
your head, your heart, your skin, your spirit
like the ocean pulling at the shore.
I swath my rag doll body over yours,
hook you in woolen arms, button you all over me,
zip my fingers up your spine,
squeeze muscles, breast, belly, heart to your heart,

pray that the shrouds of Mary
bundle illegible cells,
squeeze and poop and spit them right out of you,
make this plague
pass over, pass over.

I mark you with an X,
my swaddled girl, and
from prone body beg the Almighty
to pass you over, pass you over
so together we unzip, rip, and cross this cancerous Nile.

# Arguing in the Radio-Therapy
   Waiting Room

Pointless, you say,
just like
petunias or poinsettias or pansies
the time I waste on them
there is nothing
to talk about.
You pull a strand
of loose hair,
dead, you see.

A real
teenager,
I say.
Pink checkered cap sucks
in retreating
eyebrows
palpable scars buried beneath the bank
river-sized t-shirt, pink hearts and cool dude
hangs like bushy hair
pants swimming in currents about the hips
earphones streaming hard rock
like crushing stones to me
words slide
under a waterfall
of adolescence.

At the call of your name
you turn
just like every other
teenager, except you
for radiation
you hand me your cap.
I pass the wait-time
pulling the loose strands
caught in the cotton.
I let them
float
to the
floor
the way
drizzle spits up
spits back
just feet away
from the waterfall.

# Girl in Tulips

A moon night-light shone about your head
beamed at the Madonna strapped to your bed-frame.

A nurse tiptoed among horizontal forms
in the flickering coin-glow of her miner's headlight
checked your heart beat, blood pressure on beeping
flashing red screens, and pressed the reset button
with a hand that could have wound Dali's melting gold clocks.

Her contorted science made of you a Matisse's Odalisque
a lone woman splayed on a drab bed in a wide empty space—
the one I dragged you away from *au musée*—or
a Picasso's twisted female triangle—the one where man is ripe—
all those God-damned women-snatching copycats
as if you were born to hang on someone's wall or in glass display.

The flashing red screen graphs the pulse
but not what put it in motion:

Chestnuts your ancestors plucked
in the calm of cold nights;
pasta dough kneaded by hand
of semolina wheat the color of gold;
the arch of your grandmother's brow now yours,
olives the color of your skin
from trees on oasis of hills.

When I finally get you home
I wrap you in tulips upon white cotton
between three petal lips
you as the pistil growing inside.

# Lemons

I can't make you believe.
Lemon is a fruit, an acid,
an acid fruit you hurled at me.
Lemon juice you squeezed from ripe lemons down my skin,
You scrubbed till I bled red acid, still not yellow,
grated away my rinds, swirled them into cakes you gave away.

> I can't tell you
> how you only tasted the sour lemon in me,
> how you made me want to cut myself,
> squeeze myself out, become a real lemon,
> how I just wanted you to love me
> for my greasy olive skin even if it never shone bright
> but deep like the earth, how you said lemons cut grease,
> how I belonged in the pit of it.

I can't make you believe
how I want to shine a globe sun lemon,
a yellow gemstone lemon, radiating from the sun,
how lemon scent fills an empty, airless soul,
how its blossoms attract the sun,
how lemons sweeten the tongue.

# Gemini Splits into Cancer,
# Disputes with Leo

# Every Part

Every week I hauled you
back to the gray garage, the clown mechanic,
back to the dull blue greased gray hydraulic altar,
   your hand, cold as metal, unlocks from mine as you lift up.

They inspected electro-lights pale as the Holy Ghost,
redeemer diagnostics: thorned valves, sparkless plugs, timing belts
gone mortal, the soft beam on your radio extinguished,
   each part, a part apart.

Every day I salvaged your engines,
shepherded spirits into tubes till imbibed, offered communion
by spoon to empty tanks at vespers, kept vigil on your dimming dashboard,
   scraped oily offal spills off floors.

Almighty med students came to test drive
steer the wheel for a while, take an intercessive spin,
your feet black as tire treads,
   ankles swollen like the dirty Rock Creek swallowing the park.

Every time I was Abraham, the perfect devotee,
hauling the lamb child up the mount to the slaughter,
pressing a knife to your beloved throat,
   pleading God the Almighty to provide.

# Honeysuckles

Blood drips through vines directly to your vein
where you begin in a white sea-bed and I end in your eye
tendril tubes stretch to depths far beyond
membranes of our honey-scented patio where

honeysuckle vines twine around the wooden railing
trellis patterns intricate in their own designs
round up fence and yard to where
yellow-horned homes for honey bees and palisade hold each other.

Some stranger you will never meet blood-let
intricate trellis blood patterns to flow into your vein-vines
winding round to where your blood can hold on its own
and where the blood I gave you and all I can do as a mother end.

# The Intruder

I did not expect
this chocolate croissant. Who left it?
Is that what you call stuffed with cream,
wrapped inside dull, parched flakey flatulent mica,
fat-fed dough drooping at its sides
as if sun-scorched where burnt skin
peels back to reveal wafers
of pink scabby skin, disembodied at one greasy touch?

I never ordered this lump of lard
not filled by the hands of a practiced pastry chef
not kneaded by diligent dessert apprentices
but born of chemical salt baths,
names no grocery shelf will read,
captured under plastic.

Oh lifeless, scum bun pooped out by
industrial assembly line intestinal tract,
you call yourself *Pain au chocolat*, wait wordlessly
in the kitchen corner for punished moms, but why?
Are you a calorie bomb meant to keep my mouth busy, busy, not bitter
so I may rejoice at sweet ease of reach?
An oracle are you, saying *taste the new world, chew away,*
*don't watch the silent spectacle of needling, prodding, doping children,*
*just stuff, swallow the doctor's diagnosis?*

I never wanted to wade into this corner kitchen cubicle,
never asked to sit across from you, pompous leech,
never imagined a sterile stove,
scrounging for spiritless spiked coffee or tissues,
never wanted to meet other cast-away moms,
now, now not only must we share this sacred space,
we must see eye to eye.

# Forgiveness

Between white walls and starched white coats
ghosts tread and whisper, *stay with us.*

Sins have arrived here:
hastily spat remarks I wish I could erase from your memory,

spankings from a hand too swift for its own good,
the denial of dessert for poor eating.

The mother collapsed on the floor outside of her
four-year old daughter's room,

the boy whose leg then life were amputated,
his mother ate from the other mothers' plates in the kitchen.

The ten-year old Brazilian girl who shared a room with you,
her ringlets filled more of the bed than she did,

her father had all the faith his cross could give him,
the boy who walked out then was wheeled back in,

his parents painted pictures of angels on his wall.
*Will you still be my mother in heaven?*

He cried whenever she got up to use the bathroom.
The day before he went cold, he watched

his younger brother play in the thawing playground
while his aunt and grandma wept in the hallway.

I turn a stone ear to those ghost whispers,
steer white coats by the arm, beg forgiveness.

*Do not ask, I am coming right back,*
*because I am still your mother.*

# Beautiful Scar

Big, beautiful scar,
how lovely you are
long, rufous wormy thread
climbing up my baby's head.

Windy ruby rose twine
Stitched up my baby's spine.
Not Humpty, not Dumpty,
nothing like Frankenstein.

Big, bold, beautiful scar,
you are my black star.
She's alive, she's alive!
She will thrive!

A star sewn so bright
to parents' post-op delight.
Knobs, nodules, perfect pink points
holding inside my baby's joints.

She's alive, she's alive!
Oh thank you, little black star,
how big, bold, beautiful you are,
oh lovely scar, oh lovely scar!

## Olive Oil

In hand-me-down pots olive oil boiled,
splattering off the white-haired woman.

*Ecco,* she said,
passing me the bottle:

*This is how you do:*
*pour, stir.*

Her hands large as the spread of leaves
knobby knuckles of olive trunk knots,

garlic-smeared fingers, baby zucchini,
skin of slow-cooked pepper, she

splashed in offspring, fried them up,
stirred with a splintered wooden spoon.

*It's your turn now,*
*show me how you do.*

# Cicada

If you do not steal away from that cold chamber,
if healing orbits toward the sky rather
than show its hide to the sun,

    or splits its draped thread from

the crescent of the thin moon,
you would miss a second
sun's spotted cycle on your arched path.

The cicadas at the feet of oaks will measure
your light treads on their abandoned armor,
they'd dig from their slumber

    —sing your serenades.

This is only a slice. I will have to beat on cicadas' drums,
ride out their solar radio waves calling you back
from the molted you

    I keep from sticking to oaks.

# Diamond Buds

Diamond hair buds burgeon on golden scalp,
a constellation of sisters and stars
congregate in a galaxy of generations
flocking from farms and villages

to cities, pumping gas, buying milk
in plastic at $1 a container and bleached,
bread preserved in bags, ingredients we can't name,
jobs moved across continents, machines replaced us.

Doctors stab girls with needles
eyes can stretch miles before meeting green
playgrounds—concrete-prison cells for prey.
Safety plays video games in living rooms,
children contract leukemia, and no one bats an eyelid.

Lambs drink recycled water from a faucet.
Diamonds bud on your head
refract the light by day
reflect the darkness at night.

# Autumn

# Dragged

I dragged you again to the doctor's
pulled a silent horse nodding its head up and down
past the gapping hole in the excavated backhoed asphalt
past the boarded Thai restaurant
through snakes of cars toiling past billboards
bearing computer-generated images of new apartment
complexes and trees whose tippy-tops barely reached the second floor
past grocery stores of products no one ever needs
ads of open-mouthed plump women in skimpy clothes

Heads nodded past
the noose hung loose around our necks like gold
I let a doctor stick needles into your arm
a mother who worshipped
modern medicine as a goddess
you were silent as a horse awaiting its rider
by the time the needle was removed
the three heads of Cerberus surrounded you in the shadows
Hades in the white coat was telling me not to look back.

# Fishmonger Girl

Each day she put down her red backpack
next to the dirtying, graying waters
of the fishbowl, the red goldfish fluttered
around the plastic plant
rippling its threadbare fins
its dog lips salivating,
eyes orbiting within saucer sockets.

The girl's hand at the top of the tank
brought the fish up upon its own undercurrent
gasping for air and feed like the Last Supper
winged fins flurrying woodpecker flurries under water
till satiated and zapping through the tank
circling the plastic plant on its fish orbit
as momentous fish tank fish do, till lulled by sleep.

Every ten seconds of the goldfish's turns,
I wished you, my girl, as a fish-be in blue-gray waters
of hospital bed tank,
rippling a current, commanding water,
slippery, sleek, scaled so chemo ripples slip away,
wishing it fluttered right off, you swimming through
slicing water with fins, gulls stealing breaths.

For the months your red backpack sat next to the tank
the comings and goings, the meds, the blues of your bed, the bills,
we orbited you like the sun, our goddess,
watched you withering, wilting, shriveling,
stretching, blooming, blossoming cycles of toxic treatments
while the red goldfish
fixed its orbiting eyes on your red bag
gulped, ballooned, and bellied up.

# Inkblots

Organs flashed up on a screen
up close and singular
the brain an oversized walnut
plum moon eyes orbiting Saturn
your heart a feathered hoof
pounding on the barn door.

These *clichés*[1] remind me
of you on your horse,
oddly enough:
the gray strobes of the screen
like graying-white wind rummaging your hair
your eyes focused ahead
a wild whip gripped but lingering idly
the horse following your gaze instinctively
your eyes piercing out the direction even though
the horse can't see you over its ears
its trust in your foresight.

You refuse to look at your own milky innards
but I stare at the varying gray-scaled screen,
the reflection of my own face in the glass gazing back at me.
Horses and women suffer in silence when they take ill,
now I point the way ahead with my eyes
and you from in front follow instinctively.

---

1    *cliché* means x-ray or MRI image in French

# Send out the Clowns

First we heard them down the corridor
    Phoebe and I, squirreled away in her secluded room.
*Don't let them in*, she pleaded.
    Down the hallway the trio troubadours
        were banging and clanging,
        flipping and flopping,
    red noses and pink polka-dotted cheeks of them
in blue-green suspenders
slapping tambourines, the flippedly-floppedy trio troubadors
    'n signing opera 'O Solo Mio' and clickety-clacketting
    in wooden-heeled cowboy boots and oversized shoes,
    they inched closer, wide-mouthed, slit-mouthed,
oh no, they were dancing and prancing,
swinging and sashaying up to her double-glass door
    smiling and slapping, chuckling and waving

*Don't let those clowns near me,*
    Phoebe pulled the covers up to her chin
    they were waving and tapping and banging and clanging
the tambourine trio, one woman and two men, frolicking,
    singing and tooting a horn now, the noise of ten
the glass doors slid open, Phoebe sank into her bed
    *Send out those clowns!*

In they glided, Phoebe shrieked
    but they were banging and clanging, tooting a little horn too,
    tapping and rapping, hitting tambourines on their hips,
    swinging and swaying
    dancing in circles too
and jumping and singing and pinching and slapping each other
    Elvis' sprang in the air from their lungs.

Phoebe sprang upright in her bed,
  *send them away, send them away*
they sang 'Blue Suede Shoes' till Phoebe shrank
again in bed and cried

suddenly Elvis tripped on his blue suede shoes
    and held his breath
      the tapping tapped out, and the rapping rapped out
the clanging went bang and the bang went clanging
    and the swinging and swaying went still
      the little horn bleated a last hoot

    and they waited with downturned grins and real tears
    and clambered softly on their tambourines
    watched her face and turned to me
Then Phoebe shouted, *tell them, Mom, tell them!*
    so they fixed their daze at me, their hands mid-air
      tears mixed with red, pink, white streaked their faces,
I held Phoebe's hand in mine

*Tell them, tell them!* Phoebe pulled her covers up.

So I looked at the trio tambourine clowns
    right in their over-outlined, pigmented eyelids
    right in their tear streaked make-up
    right in their red plastic noses
—skipped smelling the white carnations on their red lapels—

*thank you*
*Ms and Mr Tambourine Clownsters,*
I inhaled and exhaled
*thank you,* my chest expanded
*—for—for frightening my daughter*
*more than her own illness.*
*You can go now.*

44

# Flock

Sheared sheep must not mingle with the flock
until every single one has been sheared.

The lady farmer dons gloves for the shave,
directs clipped woollies through a gate.

My younger daughters bid me to braid their flowing hair,
one tells her sister to choose a single plait.

Their shorn sister hides upstairs in the bathroom,
rubbing "no tear" baby shampoo onto her scalp, eyes awash.

Sheep abandon the lamb that falls to the wolf,
huddle to keep warm in the cold after the lamb is gone.

# Angels of Fury

Angels of fury sucked my cherubim into Hell city
spewed bisphenol, neonics, aluminum salt through her veins
burst the dam of perfect blood cell round.

I am whipped at this altar of truth,
left to trace blanched contours around whitened eyes,
wipe sweat from cold temples, hold cups to bleeding gums.

Those pale contours, the wrinkles of pain embedded in skin
reflected in viewing mirrors at gas stations,
in plastic bottles in park trashcans, cigarettes at cash registers.

Dear Angels, build a rotunda to replace those wings,
light a torch for her circle of life, bring saffron for the cocktail
elderberry jam before the bleed, offer jenever before the inferno.

The Angels of Fury kicked open the gates, fueled the flames,
Tisiphone pried you by your head, Alecto and Megaera
secured me by the waist as I strapped my hands around your ankles.

# Windfall

Will your spirit be forever frozen in the yard
where you fanned angels in the heavy snow?

Will winter's child join you to the choir of seraphs
trumpeting hailstones down on the rooftop?

Will warming weather lift you
up staircases you wobbled to climb?

Will the wind blow prayer-hand pine cones into my palms
like postcards from heaven, pictures of places we'd rather be?

Will I still be your mother?

The neighbor's black cat you invited over for coffee
drank milk from your baby bowl.

Will I beg kitty to tune into a higher frequency
tap messages of retreating clouds?

Will she call on the rectory for holy water
entreat all saints to keep you with me?

Bastet jumps on our windowsill meowing from thirst
a phial of oil hangs from her collar.

# Winter

# Milk Line

A tube connects you to bottle of milk
North Star hanging above your head
the dim glow of lights on the pump casts rays
about your room like the church nativity scene at night.

The pump beats a rhythm.
Another type of tube once connected you to me
your heart beat softly inside my nativity scene.

Though I feel replaced by this new lifeline of yours
this fishing rod drudging you from the ocean
this cocktail between abyss and your new neon star

I praise Mary for it.

# Three Wise Men

Three wise men
Christmas ornaments bob over her head
hanging from the star pole.

Gift-bearers:
CISplatin, Cyclophosphamide, Domustine
hovering saints' statues on cathedral facades

Nurses in green-caped
gowns and sealed gloves grasp
glowing myrrh and frankincense, price of gold.

Trees in the courtyard
stare through filtered floor-to-ceiling windows
lights reflect off the plastic sealed pouches

Pocked-faced
dripping yea-sayers by modern science
drop your hair like pine-needles from a dry branch

your skin turned three hues
yellowish-orangish gold, color of garden lights
auras reflecting pollution over the earth.

Plastic Christmas trees
render extinct the slaughtering of pines.
New-fangled life-saving hunters, killers, invaders

Bring us down on our knees
before these three new kings.

## That Sarah Should Speak

What did Sarah say when Abraham marched their son up the mount?
Did she hear the usual catch-phrase from her spouse: *o, just taking a little*
  *walk up the hill with our boy, dear*, or something less ceremonious?

Abraham never told Sarah that he pressed a knife to their son's aorta.
  Did they know aortas then?
The son whom she laughed about having, the one she had in
  advancing years.
Did Sarah wait for an angel to bring him back?

I waited years to have you, bent on knees before the statue of Mary.
No one ever told me to sacrifice you, never said you'd be an offertory
  lamb on a grill. Still, you were charco-broiled, zapped under radiating
  wings playing God, till you were a certain sacrifice.

I kept screaming, I kept screaming; *no, not my baby girl! Not my baby girl!*
I kept screaming and crying and throwing up a ruckus, and nobody
  could say anything except, *hold on, hold on!*—not to let you slip
  through the tsunami of treatment so that I could have you
nailed, painted, recharged, and set next to me like Isaac on the altar
and the Madonna with her own Christ child.

Did Sarah say something like that, too, or something even more
  unceremonious?

# Christmastime

Church bells ring out
Their hallowed tones reverberate
From merchant to office walls
From cold stones
Its swinging loose tongue clapper
Calls for rejoicing or dread, maybe it does matter.
People coagulate in the cobblestone square
Their throats wrapped in heavy scarves
Their bare crowns open to bell throated bottoms
Their coattails swag like feathers lifting in winds.
They call to toddlers chasing pigeons
Not to kick the birds in the beaks.

# Ward Moms

*Respire, respire, ça fait mal, mais ça va passer.*
  *[Breathe, breathe deep, it hurts, but it will pass.]*

  Mothers camp in the small ward kitchen
  pitch plastic cups of emptied coffee or black tea
  hunt rule-conforming groceries stocked in the sterile fridge.
  On the far side of the window, beyond the pane,
  waning trees willow in the wind. In blue metallic
  beds down the hall children incubate
  infused with nuclear medicine.

    *Respire—respire profondement—ça descend, ça descend.*
      *[Breathe, breathe deep, it's going, it's going.]*

Ward mothers sort energy-laden foodstuffs from homemade left-overs,
discard recent from more recent, before the nurse does it for them.
Fluorescent lights illuminate deep circles, hallowed eyes,
swollen lids lifted long enough to question
how each one was, how long each was in for, what the name was again.

    *Respire profondement, ça descend dans les bras.*
      *[Breathe deep, it's going down into your arms.]*

  Names of children one might never meet
  are displayed on trays of meals untouched,
  dishes carried from distant homes
  pour out of plastic containers
  and pile into the oven to arouse unlikely appetites.
  One mother unwraps chicken, lights the fire,
  turns to moms at the table,
  asks if gas mark 4 means 180º celsius.
  Someone pulls out her iPhone
  daylight breaks over the stove.

*Respire, respire, ça descend dans les jambes.*
  *[Breathe, breathe, it's going down into your legs.]*

She says maybe it should be gas mark 6,
no another says, *it will burn,*
*no burn comfort food, no burn!*
We crack the shells of ourselves, laugh till tears
pearl down our cheeks,
to see food as comfort
if we keep cooking and baking,
like keeping campfires lit in await
of the return of the hunt.
We squeeze each other's hands
while uneaten meals waft their two-scents' worth
from under metal lips on trays left on the trolley.
Then the French nurse, the one who usually holds
our sweet-peas' and pumpkins' hands needle-side,
comes to yell at us
to be considerate of the sleeping children.

*[Breathe,   breathe,   you see,   it's going...*
    *it's   almost   gone]*
*Respire,   respire,   tu vois,   ça passe...*
    *ça passe...*

## To Witness Ambulances

Disco ball strobes circled the dance floor, flickering at regular
   intervals, but where were you? In the glinting darkness, I spot you
   on the wooden dance floor flamingo-ing like an ostrich, feet sliding
   back and forth, your belly doing something, your head bobbing
   forth and back.

The strobe lights and sharp sirens snapped us alert and strapped us to
   the windows. The engulfing noise. Where was it? Then you inside,
   rushing you to lady redemption. Resuscitating tubes and fluids and
   veils of blood extracted, one to replace the other. Injecting coffee
   to stare awake.

When I see sirens, like rolling discos, I think of dancing to be alive,
   the earth circling to music that gravitates us together; you at the
   center, how we created the need for blood-giving and eggs, how
   we must choose the flickerings we hold onto, like savoring the last
   dregs of cinnamon soya latte between our teeth or damning the
   cup for running out of coffee.

# No, No You Don't, Not Another Roadkill

Don't tell me about your 81-year old dad who got it, too,
    his trembling hands, his dribbling mouth,
    he survived or didn't, his struggle, his doctor.

Don't tell me about your 69-year old mom
    or your 48-year old cousin, knots like moons,
    the cloudy starbursts, battling planetary forces.

Don't tell me about your aunt's expired body
    before your plane set down,
    the mean-mouthed mourning cousins.

Don't cry over your cancer-ridden dog.
    You were the one who laced your yard with pesticides,
    the job you lost, the brother who didn't call.

Just say nothing, just let this moment live
    when I tell you about this place we call civilized, of unlawful
    laws, holes in the ozone, wandering pi bonds between negatives,

children who contract cancer from it all,
    falcons perched on roadside posts waiting for roadkills,
    the world drags us along by the feet as it turns its face to the moon.

# Absolutes

Some words do not belong together, like people
Some terms can not be uttered in same breath, as in pandemic
    Language is the pattern of collective thought, where is my
        mobile phone?
My less will always mean someone else's more

Stop your:

    Comparing apples and oranges

    Total and disaster—it is either a disaster or it is not
    Complete and massacre or
    Absolutely and absurd—both are already absolute and absurd
    Fossil and fuels
    School and shooting
    Separating and children
    Social and distancing
    Pediatric and oncology

    Please and Stop

# Whipped

The sun whips the morning out of bed
blinding steel blade in its mouth
rays with their serrated messengers slice the window
at the speed hope holds its stomach.

Papers, prescriptions, forms slip off the table in beats
these jagged cliffs are the shell of me where waves crash
smash and spit, our dollop house totters on the edge
the roof cracked, salt soaked, planks splintering.

Coffee the color of washing water stagnates
in a cup hundreds of lips have so far grazed
the handle so many idle hands gripped and quivered
white coats swoosh on by. Emptiness is its own universe.

Scouring the stockroom for a scalpel to cut myself,
while the nurses take their tea break, I wish I were a brawny drunk,
stupid believer, some opium addict who oozed in, sputtered down
dazed, dumbfounded, tagged as unknown, weaponless soldier

shipped off to the ozone, sucked up by any unidentified spaceship.
Do as the doctor says.

# Science Project

Wrapped in a purple turban, she paraded
yellowed eyes over the viewer
of the school microscope, scrutinizing
prayer-hand-shaped leaves

splayed onto slides, pulled taut
cartographic veins cut in autopsy,
vast lattices mapped in crystal light,
a world revealed in innocent crevices.

The hospital made you their science project
multiple pairs of viewing eyes
scrutinize blood-smeared slides
a map of the world unfolds.

# Invigilators

The womb that sheltered you
the milk that nourished
the lullabies that did not lull you to slumber

distant dreams now
all I can do is rub your feet
hold your cold hands

kissing the booboo has not made it better

# Aries Rams Into Easter

# Aries Head-butts an Easter Egg
## While Awaiting Easter

Walnut halves mirrored
       side by side
symmetry—even if wrinkly—in a husk

so as in the freckled face
       in arched feet
in mapped hands
       in dimpled knees
in waxing hair and
       waning moon

flashed images of your brain show
       its dimpled synaptic symmetry
contours, ventricles, secret channels,
       celestially snug in a shell,

long-tongued iris bees court sunflowers,
       then honey dance right by
even that
       is beauty in a shell.

# Grandma Puts an Egg in a Vegan Recipe

All my thoughts should be children
watch them grow, falter, flourish
travel, then choose a dowsing rod
find water, spray paint a blank
on bland buildings
mushrooming around town
on sign posts
climb trees
have children of their own
say, here's another thought
watch it play
watch it drink, eat
watch it spill milk
but don't come to me for a sponge

# Cancer Moms

Soccer moms rise like the sun, a leg at a time, then in bursts. They spike toothpicks between teeth, pat hair into place, pencil eyeliner around hazy eyes, lay layers of pale foundation over their face, nudge kids out of beds and into bathrooms, throw laundered sports bras and uniforms onto beds. They skip down to the kitchen, light the kettle for coffee, fill stainless steel thermoses.

Cancer moms rise stealth during the night, flick on flashlights, check levels of remaining high protein milk in feeder pumps and record amounts imbibed into a notebook next to the date and time; pull on a clean shirt till they remember the hour, return between cooled sheets, repeat.

Soccer moms fry eggs between parting and braiding hair and texting other sport moms, pack cheese sandwiches, potato chips, blankets into picnic baskets, instruct spouses to load cars with balls, bottles of water, folding chairs reminiscent of safari tours, binoculars, video cameras.

Cancer moms pop sublingual anti-nausea meds into cherry-sized mouths, clean feeding tubes by injecting bursts of water, wipe warm washcloths over pasty faces. Wake sibling soccer kids and throw clean soccer uniforms and sports bras onto their beds.

Soccer moms honk by the neighbors', pick up and pack additional kids into the SUV till it brims with air, water, fire, and earth, then plan upcoming pick-up and drop-off times with other moms for practice dates. One soccer mom with dark hair swings by cancer kid's house, puts cancer kid's siblings in the back seat, waves to the soccer-n-cancer mom.

Cancer moms wake cancer children, streak toothbrushes through tight jaws, slip in mouthwash, make spit, repeat; hold sack-of-bones children over a toilet, rub lotion onto sandy skin. Streak another across the other children's teeth, repeat.

Soccer moms instruct soccer coaches on moves, flick open and press video, cheer and pump fists in the air, screw open thermos of coffee, pass around store-bought cupcakes, upload pictures onto their choice of social media. They clap during awards ceremonies, watch their daughters slide tri-color medal ribbons around their necks, congratulate coaches, hug other moms, repeat until loss occurs when they pass hugs around like donuts.

Cancer moms carry kids and bags from cars to hospital corridors, take instructions from nurses while cheering from bedsides, rub feet, kiss toes, oil bald scalps, soothe arguments from bored siblings. Hold other cancer moms' hands in the lunchroom, spoon applesauce into their other kids' mouths. Clap for the clowns when they play Elvis on ukuleles all the while wanting to hurl applesauce against white, sterile walls. They scream down abandoned hallways, suck deep into their bones secrets that no one wants to hear anyway, click and give thumbs'-up to soccer moms' social media pictures.

These all are gold-plated octopus moms, bitten at the neck, seared and branded, made of the stuff minted in kids' sport medals and nutritional packs. Children from across the zodiac spectrum are their children.

# Weavers

Green and yellow weavers weave their basket nest
Suspended in threads from acacia branches

the sun tethers the galaxy
at the tippy tail of the Milky Way

That fiery home breeds fledglings and squawking
twined by batting of wings

bickering and beaks, clamped by claws
White tight knit technicians in smart

medical coats, degrees plastered on fibers,
reweave your tissue, stretch the fabric

of your being under synthetically woven
head scarf and bandages, all the bickering

of wants resourced and rerouted
Weavers weave green and yellow

plumage into their haven
till birds and nest are but one inseparable family

# Demi Lavato Sings Us Taps

How divine to hear Demi sing us Taps
For our lost colors, white stars, and red stripes
Our families are broken and strapped
Among fragments of stained glass and burst pipes
Alongside houses swamped from pouring cloud
Young doctors labor to revive failed breath
Illicit militias play war in woods, proud
Unmasked, they pretend to ward off death
Yet Demi sang for our fallen spangled banner
And reached out to an adoring teenage girl
Wrapped in a burgundy scarf, in quiet manner
At the base of the stage, her face beamed a pearl
Holy Demi took her hand as the band played
and shared sweet suffering and tender serenade

# I Want Cake

Cake
is all I want
of ancestral Egyptian spelt,
Demeter descended, within wispy chaff
speared like Roman warriors, god-gifted
Cleopatra on the Nile where they could eat cake,
wise like winds that swept the plains, swept the seed.
And you, my sweet descendent, gift of goddesses' seed
I planted on this earth, seed that sprouted across the plain,
golden like fields of spelt, fermented in foreign wind,
I wish you all the icing.

# Effervescence

I.

The tippety-tips of the pink scarf flutter behind her, blowing in
puffs of wind generated by movement. The teenaged girl totters
toward the bus stop feet slapping the pavement, clickety-clacking,
perfectly unaware, free to herself. No one considers what hides
behind the drapery, more veils we wear when our will to live is
stronger than the physical.

That tail-tip billows out like a dollhouse curtain, the very fringe
catches a faint gust and break-dances in the air, its contents not of
its own mind, its raison *d'être* a mask but no matter.

Puppets pulled on string always smile, always smiling, a lipstick
smile, even when insults hurl their way and puppet-brooms strike
at their doll arms. I want my doll-girl to smile, defy stares, stare
back in starers' eyes.

My eyes follow the bearer's bowed head till the effervescent scarf
floats as if alone and detached, the sway of a drunk-on-life, a kite
thrust so high that its strands are no longer visible to the naked
eye. We all know that a hand firmly anchors the string to this earth
though the winds get enough edge to think that their spirits design
the whippety-whips of flight.

I crank my neck to watch—make sure of what though?—riveted to
my stake in the sidewalk, till the scarf rounds the corner on its own
cloud like when cats come around to our door, hungry, meowing,
whisking their tails straight up wrapping their soft furry souls
around her legs

just for the sweet scent of seeing her.

II.

Our kids are ventriloquists, we parents the dummies that hang over
their knees. Watch how we plunge to dirty floors on all fours
when our babies drop their favorite spoons or figurines or beanies.
Watch how we crawl under tables, stick our hands under couches
amid dust and dander, grease or oil, to retrieve Minnie Mouse
smiles or to soothe shrill screams till sanitized Minnie returns to
sticky hands.

Watch us dangle from strings getting babies into bed, curtains
drawn, lights low and babies want suckers. "Dear blessed of blessed
mothers, safe-guard our children, keep them safe from harm."

Fast-forward into the future, and their cries flash across our screens,
not to ask how we are—not to ask if we would like a slice of the
cake that they just posted on Instagram (the only medium we have
left to actually see our kids and the friends they hang out with).
No, no, I am not going to answer—no, not this time. I am going to
enjoy my dinner. I am going to finish my soup, even if the phone
sits next to my bowl.

No, they ask for cash or how much soap goes into the laundry
machine, how long it takes to cook a chicken leg. Or to accompany
them to doctor appointments, sleep next to them during hospital
stays, carry their bags, sit next to them during chemo sessions. No,
Kahlid Gibran, our children really are our children. Their pain,
our suffering. Their future, our fortune. The stunted arrows, our
brokenness.

Here it comes again, another message, signaled by the ring-tone set
just for the kids, rhyme set to beat, and there we go again. Their
house of tomorrow doesn't belong to us, but we pay their passage.

They're ours, and what are parents for anyway but to dangle on
strings as near and as far away as possible?

# Mother of the Ailing Crab

Crab kid, why have you come to me? Blue smeared and panting.
*Stop at the edge of the water. Retreat.*

*Enough from you, bossy Missy Mom.*

My daughter was born the sign of the Crab, smeared blue, curious
fugitive, profound. I wanted to make her the Sagittarius of me,
focused, hard-hooved, determined. I waiting for molting times to
grab her out of the water, to dress her myself, set her on the straight
path that she would ultimately take sideways. When she went
astray, I would grab her off the pebbled path that scraped at her
legs, toss her by my teeth on my horseback, attached her pinchers
to my mane, myself as her head. She fell each time, her soft body
caking dirt over her exposed blue flesh. I'd have to throw her back
into the water until her shell reformed, her pinchers stronger. I
stomped on her arm-pincher to hold her back from herself, but it
detached. She held it out of the water at the end of her other claw
and extended it to me as a gift, like a trophy, waving it to and fro,
and she descended deeper past the shoreline. She grew a new claw,
but it was mangled and flared.

*The seas are polluted, filled with plastic. I ordered her to molt and harden.*

*Oh stop, Mom, you can't make me look in the direction you set, I can dart in
and out of the water. You will scrutinize the surface of the water, I will be
underneath, I will emerge at a point where you cannot imagine, where you
cannot go. I can live in two separate and incompatible worlds where your
thoughts do not linger. You thought that the hoof of your mighty horse leg,
the weight of your horse body, could trample me, pinch my pincher to trap
me. I have released it, I grow another, I re-molt, I harden, and emerge. Now
I keep one eye on you and the other on what I want.*

*Stand back.*

# Gifts to Myself

I want the hair of Samson, hide:
Worn, bulging willow bunches at my midriff
Blooming deliveries, a gift from God
Badge of honor for stares.

Stretch marks, endowment for bearing
Willow creepers emblem blazed deep into my skin
Gold medal for starving, shrinking to lesser scars
I want coiled locks surging from my temples.

Visible varicose veins illuminate cubic legs
Proof of bloodletting lifelines to myself
Rooibos tea pouring under palpable glares
I want blood-red beanstalk willow branches brimming from my head.

Balloon magic uterus, blown up still-life
Entrustment for conceiving neonate presents
Attracts covert glances for the flab of remembrance.
Samson shall swing, slide along my slow curves.

The "hate" rants hurled from daughter's mouth
Giggles from my mother; blessings she says
Blossoms sprouting from sprawling roots.
Samson will wind like veins around my wrinkles, lurch from my trunk.

Of these opulent weeping willow bequests
Just a parting one to myself, please:

I want the hair of Samson.
Bounce me back at each rant
Lash out at each critical eye, slap mean mouths
Fill the idle womb of *infans* or hysteria.

Let my weeping Samson ringlets whorl:
Buffer my Delilah daughter under burgeoning boughs,
Buttress her with sweeping bestowal and
Topple temples of non-believers.

# Searching for the Next Dave Brubeck

—Just You, Just Me[1]

Traveling with a teen on a country road
leading us further into the future to her university
each local radio station blurting blue and dark tones
my daughter turns the dial like a tuning fork
till the next pop song sings of lost love and foul language
indescribable and profane electrically reproduced discord.
Thoughts wander over the wheel beyond wheat fields and hills
where music brought people together
even when politics ripped them apart.
I want to turn the car around
back to the piano, the base, a real saxophone
orchestras full of color, with women and men,
but the tires keep pounding the pavement
in a discombobulated drum roll.
My young adult had already popped in ear pods
car games now only distant memories
of childhood so quickly forgotten.
Let's take five with Dave, I tell her.
*Who is Dave?* she asks.
*Who is Dave?*
Dave with oak root hands
tap dancing across the keyboard
combining clarinet with upswing bass
the welder of classical and modern
innovative and traditional, patterns and pastels
improv with big band, harmony and melody
mixer of black and white and five in four.
The crowd wild with bone-gripping fervor
and muscle moving rhythm
the car now swaying and tapping to beat

my daughter air-playing the sax
I'll pick up piano, she says,
our secret mission searching for the new Dave
time-traveling war hero, joiner of styles, colors, ages
in troubling times, the next Dave
like taking five to be together
while my daughter is the young lion
off to her own den
and I the old tiger seeing her off.

---

1   Title of an album by Dave Brubeck, as is "Young Lions and Old
    Tigers"

# Pi Day

Placates needled into pierced veins
    ancient yellow blood rivers flowing from
        beginning of womankind

from mother to baby, over rocks to oceans
    until art forms, the body is infinite
        wisdom, the water running through it

stains spread into circles on cloth
    we circle back to spots where we were born.
        They removed the bird from your chest

diamonds budded on your head
    refracted the light from the LED bulb
        brightened past intensive care

past post-op care to outpatient
    you are released
        through revolving doors

open to yourself, ruffle your wings, fly, soar,
    the sun circles through feathers
        we watch from the ground.

# Taurus Stampedes into Gemini

# Vinegar People

Here they come
    the vinegar people, all runny, sour, stringent
the question-mark noses
    their o eyes, how did we get here? the fascination with shoes
the railroad forehead, the cat mouth washing itself with its cat paw
    as if we were all diseased and radiated nuclear waste

their wanderings, no, not patients themselves
    they prefer the shots, the nuclear pouches, crushed pills mixed into paste,
we tell them, we tell them, no, no, not just for smokers anymore
Cut open a mango, plant the seed in a box of dirt in your home
    open the roof to trees, then sprout an oak, adopt an outhouse

their heads shake at the serif of their C spines, shuffle down the corridor,
    drive off in big 4x4 cars,
one head at the wheel,
        the others curled over their devices.

# Sunflower

I love this land so much—
the rolling, sun-soaked hills
the snowcapped mountains
fields of flowing wheat and sunflowers
golden doll faces and yellow-caped bees—
I buried my daughter
in a golden field
under a snow-capped mountain
and on top I planted
a doll-faced sunflower
oh, remind me
never love again

# Love Letters to a Lost Child

Baby girl
your room has been vacuumed
and dusted
clean pressed sheets
laid across your bed
your books and drawings
on the shelves
your toys, your puzzles, your dolls
in their odd places
your clothes neatly folded and stowed
in your closet
your toiletries stashed
in your toilet bag
your horse-riding medals
pinned on the walls
alongside your music posters
of smiling able-bodied and scantly dressed
singers, the jar of chocolate spread
stacked in the cabinet
all lie in waiting like princesses
should you wish to visit
come home for a spell
and let me feel you near
let me see you grimace
once more at your bedroom door
and say: *Mom,*
*'stop re-arranging my room*
*and leave my stuff alone'.*

# Survivor

My husband shoves
the local paper
in my face and says,
*look at this picture,*
*who do you see?*
As if I could see at all
Steam covers my eyes
my body slumps
over my bowl of coffee.

I want to say,
*I don't care,*
*take your damn paper*
but he insists,
points a finger.
The headline reads
"21-year old boy scout
buys and delivers older
people's groceries
during covid"
Isn't that something
I want to say
but my tongue gets
caught in my throat

Hubby holds the paper
close to my wet eyes
I examine
the 21-year old boy scout's face
yes, that's him
he looks just like his mother
her girlish round face, red hair
except with curls

when we took our kids
to the playground
chatted over pumpkin soup and pasta
I think
of all the projects
my daughter planned
and executed
I write all the headlines
the newspaper will never publish
no one will ever read:

"Girl with brain tumor raises
thousands for orphanage in Nepal
in bake-sales
the highest sum ever"

"Girl with brain cancer
teaches orphan girls in Nepal
to play netball"

"Local secondary school girl
with brain cancer
teaches art and origami
to little kids in class
at the school fair
in a scarf and flowing dress"

"Girl survivor of brain cancer
saves sand dunes in Cornwall"

"Girl survivor of brain cancer
graduates with her
International Baccalaureate
while raising money for charity,
baking apple pies"

"Girl cancer survivor
starts university
votes for animal rights
in European elections
votes only for women
on the long list of electors
while learning sign language"

"Girl with multiple brain tumors
expresses her last wishes
for women's rights
by voting only for women
during lockdown"

—oh, and, this last one—

"Girl survivor of brain cancer
graduates university
with a degree
in protecting the earth
awakes from
lockdown nightmare
marries red-haired
former boy scout
takes her seven children to playground
eats pumpkin soup and pasta"
to be written in heaven
where angels
are left
to save us.

# Talitha Cumi[1]

Oh God, if she's sleeping, wake her
If she is slipping, oh please just shake her
Wake her, please, so I may feed her
If she should drift, please just keep her
With me, take her hand and heal her,
Make her walk and breathe air in her
If she can't rise, assemble spirits around her
If she is made of matter, angels be in her
She is not ash nor dust, oh save our daughter
Do not let the ugly and mighty make us falter
These rivers must not run of blood and turpentine
All we live in is nothing but pith and brine
Oh let her rise golden from this drying earth
And leave us not as rust, not ember, nor dearth.

---

1   *Talitha Cumi* is what Christ said to Jared's daughter to heal her.
    *Talitha* means "little girl" in Aramaic. He told Jared and his wife to
    feed their daughter when she awoke.

# The Weight of Not Knowing

We strolled, my daughter and I
     Along a busy street, a lonely passing cloud
The sun a dazzling gemstone in a crisp blue sky
     Arm in arm, you my chatter-bug daughter chatting away
We went looking to dress you all up
     Suddenly you spotted a bookstore, broke loose
And ran inside, I chased after you
     But you were already done
*Hold this*, you placed an atlas, an unabridged version
     In my arms, *all the places you want to go*
You ran on, giggling, I did my best to keep up
     With the world tucked under my arm
You ran into another bookstore
     *Wait for me*, but you had already finished
*Here's another book*, but it wasn't a book
     An encyclopedia—of castles and countrysides
You dropped in my arms
     I had to balance the tomes
You kept running and finding bookstores on that twisty lane
     Placed more and more coffee-table editions in my arms
I hobbled along, creases engraved marks in my skin
     Purple bruises blossomed and grooved

You turned a corner, I lost sight of you
I couldn't walk under all that weight
Dragging so many giant reference books
     *Come back, read with me*
*Tell me what I am supposed to find in these encyclopedias*
     Why do they exist
Life's questions weigh more than all the books can answer
     What cut trees, gutted and stripped, gave them life, gave their lives
Those books scarring my arms, tearing my muscles
     While I schlepped those words

Where are you? I can't find you
        I screamed and screamed and screamed
Even when I dumped those encyclopedias in the street
            Screeching your name, searching, pleading through parched throat
The streets now deserted, storefronts rolled down and locked
            Just rare passing clouds and a darkening violet sky
I still feel the weight of all those vacant books in my useless arms
            Not even the honor of an echo to console me

# When Children Leave,
## They Take You With Them

This leaf is the size of my daughter's hand
These days fold and unfold unto themselves
Witness the death of houseplants. The palm drunk on heat,
Bent at the hip, sweeps the dirty floor.

Somewhere up above the pines, over the breathless shoulders
Of cragged mountains, where Edelweiss once grew, eagles
Fly to their eyries, feed three eaglets through fierce beaks
Rodents still robed in fur, shredded limp by limb.

In the forest below, oaks seed acorns close to their roots.

The aloe wilts and slurps over, jells away into decay
The last born eaglet starves from scarcity. In someone's garden
Rats slink and sniff, gnaw at butternut and zucchini
I heave the spoils they leave behind into the compost box.

My daughter in an overused hospital gown cries, *I want to live.*

Somewhere in town, in someone's yard
Sun on purple figs glitters gold in the Bulbul's eye
The northern wind whips the narrow membrane of milk
The lowest branch of this fig tree droops, tunnels the earth.

Women and eagles lay and hatch eggs, feed stars to youth.
We want tomorrow as fresh as newborns, as air blessed by regal oaks
The fig is actually a uterus we eat with wasps
The uterus is actually a fig we share. Oh baby girl

Every fig brings flowers, every acorn a jeweled crown,
　　*live, live, just live*

# Portable Family

(for Roger Robinson)

And if I speak of hell
Then remind me of my nonna
Who told me to carry with me
Everywhere at all times
Photos of my children, in my wallet,
Next to the bed, in my attaché case, (my phone)
On desks, the office wall, the home hallway
Across Europe, Africa, Asia, the Middle East
They will be your energy, your wisdom, she said
Their tiny faces of smeared chocolate, your treat
Their walk through the pine forest, your solace
Their toes in the briny sea, your sun.
And when the agonizing absence presses
On the brick that was your heart
Sprinkle yourself with lemon, find yourself a quiet place
Call the name of the missing one
Picture pine trees and draw her standing there
Draw her with her toes in the briny sea
With outstretched hands surrounded by her children
Then draw her children, her diplomas, her garden
And that will be your heaven.

# Title Index

# First Line Index